Emergency! Emergency!

Written by Amelia Marshall

Illustrated by Dan Bramall

W

FRANKLIN WATTS

LONDON•SYDNEY

Flashing lights and sirens wail –
NEE NAW! NEE NAW!
NEE NAW!

The vehicles get ready with a ROAR, ROAR, ROAR!

AMBULANCE

7708

POLICE

POLICE

Big, red fire engine with
TURNING big, black tyres,
charging through the busy
streets to put out all the fires.

Police car **SCREECHES**,
the sirens blare away.
EMERGENCY! EMERGENCY!
Make way! Make way!

Speedy police bike
ZIPPING really fast,
ZIG-ZAG ZAGGING
with blue lights flashing past.

Quick! Quick!
The rescue plane
is RACING through
the sky,

climbing through the clouds, flying way up high!

Airport fire rescue truck
is waiting on standby,
HEAVING
hefty water tanks
while all the planes
fly by.

Snow rescue vehicle **CHUGS** across the **Snow**, pushing through the ice, **Hurry! Hurry! Go!**

18

Creak, creak, groan!
Rescue truck is ready.
HEAVE HO, HEAVE HO,
steady, steady, steady!

NEE NAW! NEE NAW!
Blue lights are FLASHING.
Hurry out the way,
the **ambulance** is dashing.

Lifeguard van is on patrol **up** and **down** the beach.

Driving over sand and surf,
no one is out of reach!

GUARD

Lifeboat to the rescue!
CRASH! CRASH! CRASH!
Jumping over bumpy waves,

Splish! Splash!
Splash!

Chugga! Chugga! Chugga!

Big propellers chopping!
Helicopter hovers —
it rescues without stopping!

Now all is safe and all is calm,
the emergencies are done.

The sirens slowly stop their noise,
lights out now, one by one.

Emergency terms

Siren – loud sound to warn people to move out of the way.

Propellers – blades that go round to help a helicopter or plane lift up.

Ladder – helps firefighters to reach tall buildings.

Hose – a tube that carries water, used to fight fires.

Wings – help a plane to lift and fly.

Motor – machine that supplies power to a vehicle to make it move.

Crane – a machine that helps lift heavy loads.

Tyres – cover wheels so they can grip the road.